The Great Thinker

Aristotle and the Foundations of Science

Titles in the *Great Minds of Ancient Science and Math* Series:

THE GREATEST MATHEMATICIAN:
ARCHIMEDES AND HIS EUREKA! MOMENT
ISBN-13: 978-0-7660-3408-2

THE GREAT THINKER:
ARISTOTLE AND THE FOUNDATIONS OF SCIENCE
ISBN-13: 978-0-7660-3121-0

THE FATHER OF THE ATOM:
DEMOCRITUS AND THE NATURE OF MATTER
ISBN-13: 978-0-7660-3410-5

MEASURING THE EARTH:
ERATOSTHENES AND HIS CELESTIAL GEOMETRY
ISBN-13: 978-0-7660-3120-3

THE FATHER OF GEOMETRY:
EUCLID AND HIS 3-D WORLD
ISBN-13: 978-0-7660-3409-9

THE FATHER OF ANATOMY:
GALEN AND HIS DISSECTIONS
ISBN-13: 978-0-7660-3880-1

THE GREATEST DOCTOR OF ANCIENT TIMES:
HIPPOCRATES AND HIS OATH
ISBN-13: 978-0-7660-3118-0

THE GREAT PHILOSOPHER:
PLATO AND HIS PURSUIT OF KNOWLEDGE
ISBN-13: 978-0-7660-3119-7

GREAT MINDS
of Ancient Science
and Math

THE GREAT THINKER

ARISTOTLE AND THE FOUNDATIONS OF SCIENCE

Mary Gow

Enslow Publishers, Inc.
40 Industrial Road
Box 398
Berkeley Heights, NJ 07922
USA
http://www.enslow.com

To my mother, Helen Gow

Library of Congress Cataloging-in-Publication Data

Gow, Mary.
    The great thinker : Aristotle and the foundations of science / Mary Gow.
       p. cm. — (Great minds of ancient science and math)
    Summary: "A biography of ancient Greek philosopher and scientist Aristotle, whose writings on zoology, logic, the philosophy of nature, metaphysics, ethics, politics, and literary criticism influenced Western thought for hundreds of years"—Provided by publisher.
    Includes bibliographical references and index.
    ISBN 978-0-7660-3121-0
    1. Aristotle—Juvenile literature. 2. Scientists—Greece—Biography—Juvenile literature.
3. Philosophers—Greece—Biography—Juvenile literature. 4. Science—Philosophy—Juvenile literature. I. Title.
    Q143.A65G69 2010
    509.2—dc22

                            2009023813

Printed in the United States of America

042010 Lake Book Manufacturing, Inv., Melrose Park, IL

10 9 8 7 6 5 4 3 2 1

Illustration Credits: The Art Archive/Epigraphical Museum Athens/Alfredo Dagli Orti, p. 109; The Art Archive/H.M. Herget/NGS Image Collection, p. 34; Tomisti, p. 66; AYAKOVLEVdotCOM/ Shutterstock, p. 59; Can Erdem Satma / Shutterstock, p. 55; Enslow Publishers, Inc., pp. 26, 45, 50; The Granger Collection, New York, p. 61; Images courtesy History of Science Collections, University of Oklahoma Libraries, pp. 8, 78; Jeannie Sargent, p. 99; Jupiterimages Corporation / Photos.com, pp. 3, 10, 32, 112; Kim Austin & Stacey Pontoriero/Enslow Publishers, Inc., p. 83; Lizzy Hewitt, pp. 24, 42; Mary Evans Picture Library/Everett Collection, Inc., p. 39; Réunion des Musées Nationaux / Art Resource, NY, pp. 13, 29; Robert Wallace, p. 42.

Cover Illustration: Jupiterimages Corporation / Photos.com.

CONTENTS

BEKKER CITATIONS

In the early 1800s, German scholar August Immanuel Bekker edited several editions of classical Greek works. Bekker's edition of the complete works of Aristotle, in Greek, was published by the Academy of Berlin in 1831. Even though the complete works filled five volumes, the numbering of the pages was sequential from the first page of the first book to the last page of the fifth. Bekker's Aristotle was laid out with two columns on each page and the lines were numbered in multiples of five.

Bekker references are the standard form for citing passages from Aristotle. In the Bekker reference, the first number identifies the page in his edition, the letter identifies whether it was in column a or b. The last number identifies the line. There have been many translations of Aristotle's works. By using Bekker references, you can find the relevant passage in any translation. Even though the exact wording may vary with translations, you can still find the ideas that Aristotle was presenting at that point in his text.

All Aristotle passages quoted here are from:

Aristotle, *The Complete Works of Aristotle: The Revised Oxford Translation,* ed. Jonathan Barnes (Princeton, N.J.: Princeton University Press, 1984).[1]

"DESIRE TO KNOW"

WHY DO THE FLAMES OF A FIRE BURN upward? Why do dropped objects fall to the earth? How do the contents of a hen's egg change into a baby chick? Why do crocodiles snap their upper jaws? Rivers flow into the sea; why do oceans not overflow? What substances make up the heavens, earth, and all living things and physical objects? What moves the stars and planets through the skies? What makes a successful life? What makes a good government? The world is rich in puzzles. Our everyday life puts them in front of us.

Our human nature is to be curious, believed the ancient Greek philosopher Aristotle. "All men by nature desire to know," he wrote. (980a 22) When a person begins to wonder, Aristotle

An engraving of Aristotle. In the oval frame you can see that he is identified with his hometown of Stagira and also as a Peripatetic. Teachers at his school the Lyceum became known as peripatetics.

held, he or she wants to find answers. Thinking people want to know "the 'why' and the cause," he said. (981a 30)

Aristotle's own curiosity was monumental. Living 2,400 years ago, he wondered about the world, humankind, and the universe. Aristotle spent his life pursuing knowledge. To understand the world, he looked for causes, examined opinions, and collected information and observations. In seeking explanations, he wanted to be certain that his answers were valid.

A philosopher, scientist, teacher, and writer, Aristotle was one of the most influential thinkers in history. Aristotle's ideas and approach to investigating nature shaped Western science for more than two thousand years. His position in the history of science and philosophy is unparalleled. He founded fields of study and furthered others. Through his lifelong research and investigations, Aristotle was trying to explain reality—all of it. He grappled with subjects as big as the universe and as small as the antennae of butterflies.

The Dutch painter Rembrandt painted this piece (Featuring the philosopher in Renaissance attire), *Aristotle Contemplating a Bust of Homer,* in 1653.

Aristotle was a philosopher. Philosophy was the Greek term for all serious intellectual pursuits.[2] *Philos* was the ancient Greek word for love; *sophia* was wisdom. Philosophy, "the love of wisdom," included a broad range of subjects. Inquiries into nature, human behavior, goodness, and the soul were among the many topics explored by philosophers.

For the ancient Greeks, the word for knowledge was *episteme*. The Latin equivalent of *episteme* was *scientia,* the root for the English word "science." For Aristotle, *episteme* had two key meanings. In one sense, Aristotle's *episteme* was an organized body of knowledge that could be demonstrated. Biology, physics, and meteorology are among subjects that we call science today that fell into this category. For Aristotle, other areas of knowledge, like political science and mathematics, were sciences, too. Aristotle's second meaning for *episteme* was the state of knowing.[3]

According to Aristotle, there were three broad areas of science—productive, practical, and theoretical. Productive sciences dealt with things produced by people. Agriculture, shipbuilding, and carpentry were productive sciences. Art, poetry, rhetoric, and theater were also produced by human activity. Aristotle wrote about some productive sciences. His *Poetics,* for example, dealt with aspects of poems from their plots and construction to comic and tragic subjects to rhythm and language. Practical sciences dealt with human behavior and action. Politics, economics, friendship, managing a household, and ethics were addressed here. Ethics is the study of moral behavior. The highest science according to Aristotle was theoretical science— knowledge for the sake of knowledge.[4] This included knowledge about the physical world, biology, astronomy, mathematics, and theology. Knowledge of planets, stars, death, fish, birds, water, and geometry were in this category. Aristotelian texts addressing theoretical sciences include *Physics, Meteorology, Parts of Animals, History of Animals, On Generation and Corruption, Metaphysics,* and more.

A page from a medieval translation of Aristotle's *Nicomachean Ethics* allegorizing Prodigality and Liberality (lavishness) in the top panel, and Avarice and Covetousness (greed) in the bottom panel. Human moral behavior is just one of the many subjects Aristotle wrote about.

For exploring *episteme,* Aristotle laid out ways to use statements and arguments to prove ideas. This field is now known as logic. Aristotle did not himself use the word *logic.* Aristotle's later followers called his writings on this subject the *Organon,* meaning the "tool." The texts of Aristotle's *Organon* include *Categories, Prior Analytics, Posterior Analytics, Topics,* and *De Interpretatione.*[5]

Aristotle's work was groundbreaking in many areas. Even when he was not the first person to consider certain studies, he was the first to write about several of them. For this, Aristotle is called the Father of Logic, the Father of Zoology, the Father of Modern Science, the Father of Biology, the Father of the Natural Sciences, the Father of Economics, and the Father of Empiricism.

Life and Times

Born about 384 B.C., Aristotle lived in ancient Greece during a remarkable period in history. His story is intertwined with the political events and the most famous people of his time.

Aristotle's adult intellectual life had three main periods. As a young man he was a student and rising philosopher in Athens. There he studied with another of the greatest philosophers of all time, Plato. In middle age, Aristotle traveled. He lived for a time in Assos (now in Turkey) and on the Greek island of Lesbos. On Lesbos, he did extensive research into ocean life—marine biology. Then he spent time at the court of King Philip II of Macedon. Some accounts claim that he tutored the king's son, Alexander, who became Alexander the Great. At around age fifty, Aristotle embarked on the third phase of his life and intellectual career. He returned to Athens and founded a school that was unlike anything that existed before. Aristotle's Lyceum was a spectacular center for teaching and research.

Learning about the life of any person who lived long ago poses challenges. Aristotle is no exception. The vast body of Aristotle's existing writing offers almost no biographical information. No stirring descriptions tell us of times with his wife and children or friends and colleagues. His surviving words offer no picturesque scenes of Aristotle buying fish from local fishermen in Lesbos or studying the night sky above Athens. We only find a few hints at his personal life in his own words.

The main source of information about Aristotle's life was written five hundred years after this giant of a philosopher lived. Diogenes Laertius in the second century A.D. wrote a collection entitled *The Lives and Opinions of Eminent Philosophers*. His encyclopedia-like volume included entries about Plato and Aristotle. Besides his account of Aristotle's life, Diogenes Laertius included a list of bequests supposedly made by Aristotle in his will, and a poem that Aristotle wrote about his father-in-law. Diogenes Laertius's account is not accepted in its entirety, but several key points in it frame the traditional view of Aristotle's life.

Fortunately, we have a wealth of information about Aristotle's ideas. Thirty-one Aristotelian treatises still exist.[6] A treatise is an article or a book. According to Diogenes Laertius's list, originally there were more than 150 works by Aristotle. Some of the texts on his list, and even some of the extant (surviving) ones, were likely written by other thinkers who worked or studied with Aristotle.

One ancient writer, Cicero, a Roman statesman and philosopher in the first century B.C., knew Aristotle's writing well. Cicero compared Plato's prose to silver and Aristotle's to a flowing river of gold.[7] This was high praise. Plato's writing is still admired for its lovely use of language. Cicero was probably describing some of Aristotle's lost works. Aristotle's extant writings offer fascinating, thought-provoking ideas, but they are not always easy reading. One poet, Thomas Gray, harshly compared reading Aristotle to eating dried hay.[8]

This contradiction between Aristotle's reported flowing prose and existing texts has an explanation. Some of Aristotle's works were intended for popular audiences rather than his students and fellow philosophers. Not technical or detailed, these were probably elegantly written. The poem that Aristotle dedicated to his father-in-law shows that he could make words sing when that was his goal.[9] Aristotle's popular texts are known as his "exoteric" works. Exoteric means that they could be understood by most people, not just an informed small group. The treatises that still exist are among his "esoteric" works. Esoteric means that they were intended for and understood by a few people who were familiar with their subjects. The esoteric works were written for the students and philosophers inside the school. Some scholars have suggested that these works were really lecture notes— outlines and basic ideas that Aristotle and others would use in classes.[10]

It is unfortunate that the style of some Aristotelian texts, or their reputation for difficulty, sometimes discourages readers from dipping into this extraordinary philosopher's words. Even though he lived 2,400 years ago, Aristotle posed valid questions and addressed meaningful issues. Aristotle's ideas and words are not like dusty relics in an old museum. A reader first approaching Aristotle may be surprised to find that he wondered about many of the same things we do today. While some of his vocabulary and references may seem daunting, readers who move past these stumbling blocks can find great satisfaction in Aristotle's arguments and observations. With a little effort, many readers are rewarded with the amazing feeling of exploring compelling and relevant topics alongside one of the greatest thinkers of all time. Aristotle still speaks directly to us across the centuries.

Greek Science

Because of their vast contributions to scientific knowledge and investigations, it is sometimes said that the ancient Greeks "invented" science. Beginning in the sixth century B.C., about two hundred years before Aristotle, the Greeks started considering the natural world in different ways than earlier people and other civilizations. Greeks began looking for non-supernatural explanations for natural phenomena. They also tried to find rational proof of their explanations. They debated and examined explanations, testing them to try to find the real reasons for natural events.[11]

A daily experience that we share with the ancient Greeks offers a simple picture of this change in perspective. Everywhere on Earth, except close to the north and south poles, the sun rises in the east and sets in the west every day. Observing the sun, it does not take long to see that it rises and sets in a predictable pattern. A supernatural explanation for the sun's passage would be that the god Zeus had a team of horses pull the chariot of the sun god Helios across the sky each day. The supernatural explanation left room for Zeus to sleep late some days or send Helios at different times. One Greek myth told how Zeus once spitefully forbade Helios to go at all. Yet, people's experience confirmed that the sun was there, day after day. They also saw how it rose and set in different positions on the horizon in a recognizable pattern that repeated year after year.

With supernatural causes, phenomena in nature were individual and random. An eclipse of the sun could happen any day the gods chose.

A wheat seed could produce an olive tree. A river could flow uphill. With order in nature, laws and principles governed natural phenomena. An eclipse of the sun would only and always occur when the sun, moon, and Earth aligned. Wheat seeds only produced wheat plants. Rivers flowed downhill.

Beyond moving away from supernatural causes, the Greeks also turned to their powers of reason to explain nature. They suggested causes and they examined and criticized each other's ideas. As thinkers scrutinized theories, they rejected explanations that did not stand up or could be shown to be flawed.

Aristotle's contributions to the development of science were monumental. He advanced factual knowledge about fields like biology and zoology. He framed questions and suggested approaches that were built upon for centuries. He showed the value of observation and collection of evidence in scientific inquiry.[12]

Today, as in the past, Aristotle can guide readers to a new understanding of dozens of subjects. University libraries have hundreds of different books about this incomparable thinker. Volumes address Aristotle's views about the human soul, politics, mathematics, art, God, women, sleep, dreams, the environment, slavery, happiness, friendship, and more. Here, we are going to take an introductory look at some of Aristotle's ideas that relate to science. Because we do not know the order in which Aristotle wrote his texts, we will first look into his life and times and then consider a few of his studies.

2

THE STAGIRITE

WHEN WE THINK OF ANCIENT GREECE, often the first place to come to mind is Athens. Athens was the home of democracy and the magnificent Parthenon and other landmark temples. A cultural center with great theater, sculpture, and art, Athens was a commercial hub and military power. Two of the three main chapters of Aristotle's intellectual life took place in that sparkling city. His non-Athenian birth and his homeland connections, however, were lasting influences on his life.

Aristotle's story began about two hundred miles from Athens. He entered the world about 384 B.C., in the Greek town of Stagira. Ancient Stagira was located in northern Greece, on the

A view of the ruins of the ancient agora surrounded by modern Athens.

Chalcidice peninsula. The peninsula's rugged inland mountains were forested in Aristotle's time. Lower land, near the sea, was farmed. Olive trees, producing one of the most important foods of the Greek diet, grew along the coast.

The ancient Greece of Aristotle's time was not a country in the modern sense. It was not a single territory defined by an encompassing boundary. Neither was it a nation organized under one government. Instead, the Greek world was made up of hundreds of self-governing communities. The Greeks called this type of independent city-state a *polis*. Each polis set its own laws and defined the rights and privileges of its citizens. Some polises were ruled by groups of aristocrats, some by a single ruler. Athens, one of the largest and most populous polises, shaped a government where citizens made decisions for their community—the world's first democracy. Democracy was soon adopted by other polises. Many polises were in the region we now know as Greece. Others were

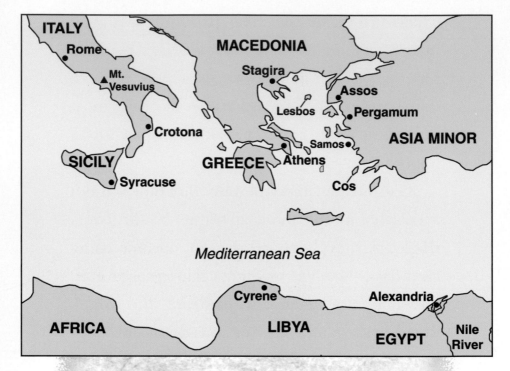

A map of Greece and the surrounding areas in Aristotle's time.

far away, in lands of modern France, Spain, Libya, and elsewhere.

The polis, Aristotle wrote, "comes into existence, originating in the bare needs of life, and continuing in existence for the sake of a good life." (1252b 29-30) The Greek polis "is a creation of nature," he said, and "man is by nature a political animal." (1253a 3) The polis was an ancient Greek's community. Goods were bought and sold in its city marketplace. Crops were raised on farms in its countryside. Men from the polis served in its military in times of war. A Greek's polis was part of his identity.

Beyond their polis loyalty, Greeks also had strong cultural identity. The ancient historian Herodotus explained that Greeks shared "our common ancestry and language, the altars and sacrifices of which we all partake, the common character which we bear."[1] Regarding ancestry, Herodotus meant that Greeks were descended from Greeks. Even those who lived in distant colonies traced their families back through generations of Greek ancestors. Greeks in their many polises spoke the same language. They called non-Greek speakers "barbarians." (Supposedly other tongues sounded like "bar-bar" to them.) Herodotus noted the Greeks' "altars and sacrifices." By this, he meant their religion. With local variations, Greeks believed in a group of immortal superhuman gods and goddesses. Ceremonies with animal sacrifices and community feasts dedicated to these deities were central to Greek community life.

Stagira was Aristotle's polis. With his fame, he became known as "The Stagirite." Just north of Stagira, including part of the Chalcidice peninsula, was Macedonian territory. At the time of Aristotle's birth, these lands were ruled by King Amyntas III. The king's palace and Macedon's capital were in Pella, about seventy miles from Stagira. Macedonians spoke a Greek dialect and believed in Greek gods. Towering Mount Olympus, considered the home of gods and goddesses, was in Macedon. The Macedonian royal family traced its history to Argos—a very ancient Greek city. Yet, some Greeks viewed Macedonians as not completely Greek.[2] This may have been partly because of their dialect.

Boyhood

Aristotle was born to a prominent family. His father, Nicomachus, was a doctor. Nicomachus served as personal physician to Amyntas, King of

A sculptor's interpretation of a young Aristotle studying a scroll.

Macedon. Aristotle's mother, Phaestis, was purportedly a wealthy woman.[3] Her family was from the island of Euboea. Phaestis owned land and houses there. Late in his life, Aristotle retired to property on Euboea that he had inherited from her. According to some sources, Aristotle had a brother and sister. While we do not have details about Aristotle's youth, from knowledge of Greek culture, we have some idea of the life of a boy of a prominent family.

The sacrifices and festivals of Greek religion mentioned by Herodotus would have been part of Aristotle's life from infancy. At the center of Greek religion were twelve immortal gods and goddesses, each with special powers and interests. These included Aphrodite, the goddess of love; Poseidon, the god of the sea; and Zeus, father of many of the deities and the most powerful god. The twelve principal deities were like an extended family who did not always get along with each other. Greeks honored their gods and tried to stay in their favor by offering gifts and sacrifices and conducting ceremonies that they hoped the gods would find pleasing. Splendid temples were built as homes for the deities. Temples were not meeting places like churches. Instead, an impressive statue of the god or goddess was housed in his or her temple.

The Greeks' festivals were community and religious events. Many were connected to the agricultural year. Demeter, the goddess of grain, and Dionysius, the god of grapes and wine, were celebrated as crops grew and were harvested. In Athens, a huge annual procession honored the city's patron goddess, Athena. In the Panathenaic festival, a new gown was carried to the goddess's statue in the Parthenon. Plays were staged, athletes competed, and boys and girls performed songs and dances at festivals.

Sheep, goats, oxen, and other animals were sacrificed in these events. Special altars for the slaughter of the animals stood near the temples, often situated where the statue of the deity could see the sacrifice. Priests followed a ritual of presenting the ox, sheep, or other creature to the god. They dripped water on the creature's

A statue of Zeus, king of the Olympian gods, in Greece. While the gods were an important part of Aristotle's culture, he did not attribute natural phenomena to them as many others did.

head, leading it to nod up and down. The nodding was taken as a sign that the animal agreed to its sacrifice. With a quick knife stroke, the priest killed it. The sacrificed animal was then roasted and celebrants feasted on the meat. These festivals brought communities together. They were also important in providing a regular source of meat to many Greeks.

A son of a prominent family, Aristotle would have studied in a school. Private schools for boys, supported by fees paid by parents, were well established by Aristotle's time. Studies fell into three areas: athletics, music, and the skills of reading, writing, and arithmetic. Boys memorized poetry, especially Homer's poems, the *Iliad* and the *Odyssey,* and learned to play an instrument such as the lyre. Greeks were serious about sports. Competitions, including the Olympics, were dedicated to the gods. Boys trained with coaches and competed in running, wrestling, and throwing the discus and javelin. Literacy had spread in Greece in the years before Aristotle. Reading and writing were increasingly

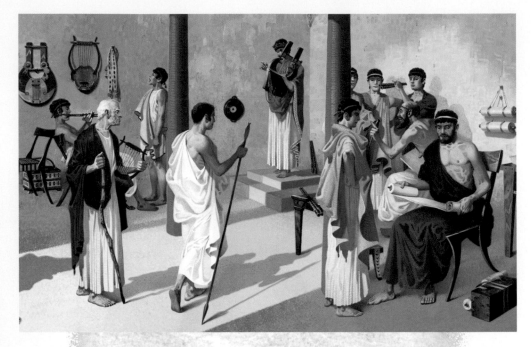

A young Aristotle would have attended a school in Stagira similar to this Athenian one. The three fields of study—music, athletics, and reading, writing, and arithmetic—are represented here by the lyre (left), the spear (center), and the scroll (right), respectively.

important to public life. Athenians wrote names of candidates on ballots, and laws were written rather than just repeated from memory.

Girls did not typically go to school, although there may have been some formal education for daughters of aristocratic familics. At least some women were literate—pictures on pottery show women reading Greek scrolls. Girls were generally expected to grow up to be wives and mothers. Their youthful training focused on household skills such as spinning and weaving.

Besides his schooling, Aristotle probably had some medical training from his father, Nicomachus. Medicine was traditionally a family business in ancient Greece, although the field was opening up to others who wanted to be doctors. Like thinkers who were seeking causes for natural phenomena, some Greek physicians looked for causes and explanations of illnesses. Greek medical writings known as the Hippocratic Collection show the emergence of rational medicine.

As a boy, Aristotle possibly spent time with his father at the court of King Amyntas III of Macedon. As the king's physician, Nicomachus may have brought his family to the palace. There, Aristotle would have met Amyntas' son, Philip. Philip and Aristotle were very close in age. Aristotle's time with his father was cut short.

Nicomachus reportedly died when his son was perhaps ten years old. Aristotle's mother passed away at around the same time. Young Prince Philip's father, King Amyntas III, died soon after, in 369 B.C. After Amyntas' death, Macedon entered a period of civil war and instability.

After his parents' deaths, Aristotle was raised by an uncle. When he was seventeen years old he left Stagira. Aristotle moved to Athens where he studied with the greatest philosopher of that time.

ACADEMY AND ATHENS

WHETHER ARISTOTLE WAS DRAWN TO Athens to study with Plato, or if he went to the city and then discovered Plato's Academy is unknown. In 367 B.C., the paths of Plato and Aristotle met and would remain intertwined for twenty years. As their association started, Aristotle was still a teenager. Plato was a distinguished sixty-plus years old.

Plato's Academy is often referred to as a school, but it was not a school in the modern sense. No examinations, degrees, or graduation were offered. Students did not enroll in classes on specific subjects. Yet teaching and investigation of ideas were at its heart. Plato and other thinkers there explored ideas together. They also taught young men. Teaching happened in informal relationships. The Academy may have functioned like a club with junior and senior members.[1]

Founded by Plato around 385 to 380 B.C., the Academy was situated a short distance outside the massive defensive wall that surrounded the center of ancient Athens. From the Academy, students had a clear view of the temple-crowned Acropolis, the high point of the city. They were not far from the bustling agora, Athens' downtown, with its businesses and government buildings.

The Academy's home was a park-like area along a small river. A grove of olive trees grew there, providing welcome shade from the blazing summer sun. Alongside the park wall stood a gymnasium. A gymnasium was like a school where young men trained in sports. Gymnasia were social and intellectual centers, where men went to talk as well as to do athletics. Plato apparently started meeting fellow philosophers and interested students at the gymnasium, and then bought or built a house nearby.

This scene shows Plato teaching a group of students in his Academy.

According to Greek myths, the park's site originally belonged to a legendary hero named Academos. Academos had a role in the early history of Athens when he helped rescue a beautiful girl who had been kidnapped. Whether Academos was a real man or not is unknown. Thanks to Plato, Academos's name lives on. The word "academy" now means an educational institution or society to promote a particular aspect of culture.

During the fifth century B.C., just before Aristotle's time, Athens emerged as the artistic, cultural, intellectual, and commercial center of the ancient world. One of Athens' supreme achievements of that era was the beginning of democracy. The word *democracy* comes from ancient Greek. *Demos* means "people"; *kratos* means "power" or "rule." Democracy is the rule of the people. Self-government by the people of Athens began to take shape in 508 B.C. As it evolved, important decisions for the polis were made by the Assembly. The Assembly was a public meeting open to all citizens. Citizens were not all the people who lived in Athens, though. Citizens were sons of citizens—a man's father must have been a citizen if he was to have these rights. Women, slaves, and foreigners were not citizens. Foreigners like Aristotle were known as metics. Metics could live in Athens but could not vote or own land there. Some Athenian citizens were rich, but many were not. Cobblers, potters, and men who rowed warships were among the city's citizens. In classical times, Athens' territory covered about one thousand square miles and included about 140 towns besides the city. Perhaps forty thousand adult men were eligible to vote.[2]

The Assembly met on a hillside opposite the Acropolis. A wall and speaker's platform stood at the front of the open-air meeting place. Speeches were made and debated there. Certain decisions required six thousand citizens in attendance for a vote. A council of five hundred citizens, called the Boulé, set the agenda for meetings. The Boulé decided what issues would come before the voters.

The Athenian Assembly met on this hillside. Members of the Assembly stood on the orator's bema, the platform at the center of the wall, to address their fellow citizens. The Athenian citizens stood or sat on benches in the open space sloping down to the left. The Acropolis, with the Parthenon and other temples, is seen in the background.

Sophists and Socrates

Within the public life of Athenian democracy, speaking skills were important. If a man wanted to make a good case for a political position he needed to convince other voters. There were prestigious jobs in government—leading armies, collecting taxes, and more. Upper-class families began seeking higher education to train their sons to be leaders of the city.[3]

A new type of teacher appeared on the Greek scene. These traveling lecturers were called sophists. *Sophist* meant "teacher of wisdom." Their subjects included mathematics, antiquities, and linguistics. Willingness to teach, rather than real knowledge of a subject, was the requirement to be a sophist.[4] Charging money for their teaching, sophists instructed sons of wealthy families.

With Athenian interest in leadership, sophists often focused on what the Greeks called *arete*. *Arete* translates to "virtue" or "excellence."[5] Sophists talked about high ideals but were sometimes criticized for hollow words. Much sophist teaching was really about persuasive public speaking. Sophists taught students to craft winning arguments. Their teaching influenced many young Athenian aristocrats.

One ancient Greek took a different approach. Like the others, Socrates was concerned with moral virtue. He believed the route to virtue was found through self-knowledge. Born about 470 B.C., Socrates lived for philosophy and eventually died for it. Unlike the sophists, he did not charge for his teaching and he did not give lectures. Instead, he talked to people directly, discoursing with politicians, young men, interested strangers, even sophists. He was often in the agora, talking and listening. Questioning people about their views, Socrates led them to self-examination. As he asked and they responded, they often saw the contradictions in their ideas. Guided by Socrates' inquiry, they frequently came away with different views than their original thoughts. This way of teaching is still practiced and is known as the "Socratic Method."

Socrates led a humble life, dressed simply, and did not seek wealth. An Athenian citizen, he served in the military when he was young and served on the Boulé when he was in his sixties. Socrates had many followers. He also had enemies. When he was on the Boulé he was the only member to vote against a procedure for the trial

Surrounded by his followers, who look away in sadness, Socrates is about to take his cup of poison. Although his life was cut short, his ideas continue to influence modern thought. The Socratic method of teaching is still used today, notably in law school.

of a group of unpopular generals. He also refused to obey an order to arrest an innocent man.

In 399 B.C., Socrates was accused of corrupting the youth of Athens and of impiety. Impiety is a lack of respect for religion. Socrates was about seventy years old. He was brought to trial. In his trial he said that his mission was to speak out, question, and search for truth. In other words, Socrates was not going to change his ways. Found guilty by the jury and sentenced to death, Socrates was put in an Athenian prison. His execution was delayed for a month because of a religious observation. During that time, his followers visited him in jail. Socrates continued questioning and discussing. When the month was up, Socrates was put to death. With dignity, he drank the poisonous hemlock brought to him by the guards.

Plato

About forty years younger than Socrates, Plato was the type of youth who might have been a student of the sophists. His parents were of distinguished aristocratic Athenian families. Well-educated, Plato was a skilled writer and capable athlete—a wrestler. He would have been a likely candidate for public life in Athens. Plato chose a different course, and the world has been richer for his choice ever since.

Plato became a devoted student and associate of Socrates—he referred to him as "my elderly friend."[6] He was with Socrates at the time of his trial and imprisonment. Using Socrates' method of question and answer, Plato wrote about virtue, justice, truth, the human soul, good rulers, and more. We still explore these subjects today and readers continue to learn from Plato's words. Most of Plato's writing is presented as dialogue with Socrates. These are not transcripts of real conversations. Socrates greatly influenced Plato, but the ideas presented in these dialogues are Plato's.

During the years after Socrates was executed, Plato traveled. In his journeys, he allegedly met with other philosophers in Cyrene (now Libya), Italy, Sicily, and Egypt.[7] When he returned to Athens he founded the Academy.

When Aristotle arrived in Athens in 367 B.C., the Academy had existed for around fifteen years. The informal teaching there was centered on philosophy, but that was a broad subject. There was a political aspect to the school. The *Republic* is one of Plato's major works. It explores justice, human nature, the ideal state, and more. Mathematics and dialectic, reasoning by dialogue as a method of intellectual investigation were also topics at the Academy.

At the heart of Plato's philosophy was that virtues were real and eternal. He believed that they were timeless and not like the material things around us. Several of Plato's dialogues give us information about his theory of Forms. Plato's abstract Forms are not located in time and space. They are things like beauty and goodness. According to Plato, earthly objects only approach the perfection of the Forms, but never fully attain it.

Mathematics offers a bit of an understanding of the Forms. If you have two oranges and add three more oranges, then you have five oranges. The addition will be true if you have two plus three elephants. While the oranges or elephants are physical things, the numbers are abstract objects that are understood by the mind.

For Plato, the physical world was a kind of imperfect shadow of the higher realm of Forms. In Plato's philosophy, objects also had Forms— Forms that enabled them to do most perfectly that for which they are intended. In Plato's dialogue, the *Cratylus,* Socrates talked with a young man about Forms. As an example, Socrates used a shuttle. A tool used by weavers to pass a thread through rows of lengthwise threads, a shuttle was a familiar object.

> Socrates: And suppose the shuttle is broken in making. Will he make another, according to the broken one? Or will he look to the form according to which he made the other?
>
> Hermogenes: To the latter, I should imagine.
>
> Socrates: Might not that be justly called the true or ideal shuttle?
>
> Hermogenes: I think so.
>
> Socrates: And whatever shuttles are wanted, for the manufacture of garments, thin or thick, of flaxen, woolen, or other material, ought all of them to have the true form of the shuttle, and whatever is the shuttle best adapted to each kind of work, that ought to be the form which the maker produces in each case?[8]

This section from Italian painter Raphael's 1509 work, *School of Athens,* depicts Plato (left) discoursing with his student Aristotle (right). Plato points upward, symbolizing his idea that reality was found in the abstract. Aristotle gestures downward, emphasizing his belief that reality resides in the physical world.

We see that Plato's idea for the Form of the shuttle is like the pattern or design for it. The ideal shuttle to weave wool, for example, is not one specific physical shuttle—it is the plan that can be used to make an infinite number of wool shuttles. In Plato's scheme, the individual shuttles are only material copies of the ideal.

At Plato's Academy, Aristotle would have discussed the Forms, as well as politics, the human soul, and other philosophical subjects. When he first arrived there he was a student of older philosophers. Remaining there for twenty years, he certainly became one of the senior associates. In Aristotle's writings he moved away from Plato's Forms. While Plato saw reality in the abstract, Aristotle tried to explain reality of the physical, material world. Although Aristotle's philosophy moved in a different direction, his lifelong work shows Plato's influence.

During the years when Aristotle was at the Academy, his homeland changed. A period of instability and war followed King Amyntas' death. Philip, Amyntas' son who was Aristotle's age, eventually won power. As King Philip II of Macedon, he began to expand his territory. He won control of Thessaly, a region in northern Greece. Then he conquered Olynthus—a city near Aristotle's home of Stagira. Olynthus had been an ally of Athens. Philip was forging an empire. He was on his way to bringing all of Greece under Macedonian control.

Many Athenians feared Philip and the expanding Macedon. Some statesmen spoke passionately against him in the Assembly. There was much anti-Macedonian feeling in Athens. Aristotle, whose father was a doctor to Philip's father, was likely suspected of ties to Macedon.

In 347 B.C., Plato died. That year, Aristotle left Athens. Why he left is a mystery. Some have suggested that Aristotle departed because he was upset that Plato's nephew, Speusippus, was appointed head of the Academy. Supposedly, Aristotle was angry or disappointed because he did not get the job. Speusippus was a capable philosopher, though, and not a poor choice for the position.[9] As Speusippus was a relative of

Plato's, his appointment may have had the practical purpose of keeping the older philosopher's property in the family.[10] Anti-Macedonian feeling in Athens also may have made the city uncomfortable or even dangerous for Aristotle. Aristotle, however, may have left Athens simply because he had other subjects to study.

4

Assos, Lesbos, and Alexander

WHETHER ARISTOTLE WAS PUSHED FROM Athens or pulled to Assos to pursue new studies is unknown. In 347 B.C., Aristotle moved to this Greek city on the east coast of the Aegean Sea. This region is in the present country of Turkey. The tyrant of Assos was named Hermias. To the Greeks, a tyrant was a ruler, like a king. By some accounts, Hermias had been a slave of a previous ruler before gaining power himself.

Hermias had friendly relations with Plato's Academy. The contents of a letter from Plato to Hermias still exist. In the letter, Plato urged Hermias to work closely with two philosophers from the Academy. With a bond of friendship between them and practicing philosophy to the

The ruins of the Temple of Athena in Assos. Aristotle settled in Assos after leaving Athens.

extent of their ability, Plato predicted good fortune for them all.[1]

Perched on the coast, Assos's location put Hermias in a precarious position between Greek and Persian lands. Tensions between Greeks and Persians were never far beneath the surface. Hermias, though Greek, had managed to stay friendly with the Persians for several years. His wealth and paid army probably helped keep the peace.

Hermias apparently welcomed Aristotle. He supposedly gave Aristotle and others, "The town of Assos to live in, where they spent their time in philosophy, meeting together in a courtyard; and Hermias provided them with all they needed."[2] A personal bond was also forged between Aristotle and Hermias. Aristotle married a young woman named Pythias, reported to be Hermias's niece and adopted daughter. Aristotle's philosophical works do not contain any personal details. However, in his writing about marriage he advised ideal ages for men and women to marry. "Women should marry when they are about eighteen years of age, and men at thirty-seven; then they are in the prime of life." (1335a 27–28) Perhaps not coincidentally, Aristotle was about thirty-seven years old when he was in Assos. Aristotle and his wife had a daughter. They named her Pythias, like her mother.

We know nothing about Aristotle's family life. In his comments on household management in *Economics,* he discussed marriage and relationships. For a successful marriage, he noted that, "dissimilarity of habits tend more than anything to destroy affection." In other words, a couple with similar habits would likely be happier. He also stated that, "husband and wife ought not to approach one another with false affectation in their person any more than in their manners; for if the society of husband and wife requires such embellishment, it is no better than play-acting on the tragic stage." (1344a 17–22)

As Pythias and Aristotle were starting married life, Philip of Macedon was changing the face of Greece. After years of balancing relations with the Greeks and Persians, Hermias entered into a treaty with Philip.[3] Philip was expanding his territory. Neighbor states who had not already fallen to him were nervous. The Persians felt threatened by the Macedonians. To retaliate for Hermias's betrayal, a Persian army set siege to Assos. Hermias was captured. He was taken in chains from his city, tortured, and crucified.[4] Aristotle, Pythias, and their daughter safely departed Assos. They moved to the neighboring Greek island of Lesbos.

Living on Lesbos, Aristotle began working with another Academy philosopher. Theophrastus, fifteen years younger than Aristotle, was from Lesbos. He became Aristotle's friend and longtime fellow researcher. Aristotle was clearly studying marine biology during this time. Many of the sea creatures mentioned in *History of Animals* are from a particular Lesbian bay. Aristotle's extant texts include an impressive body of observations and marine biology research. After just a year or two on Lesbos, though, Aristotle left for the court of Philip II of Macedon.

A modern view of the Greek island of Lesbos. Aristotle did extensive research on marine biology while living there.

In 343 B.C., according to Diogenes Laertius, Aristotle "stayed in Macedonia in Philip's court and received from him his son Alexander as his pupil."[5] Aristotle was supposedly invited there to teach Alexander, the son of Philip and his second wife, an Epirot princess named Olympias. The boy was about thirteen years old. A few years later, he would make his mark in history as Alexander the Great. Alexander would conquer lands from Greece through the Middle East and Afghanistan and on to India.

The relationship between Aristotle and Alexander has fueled speculation for centuries. How did the philosopher influence the boy? Did the boy influence his master? Nothing is known about their relationship. Some sources claim that Aristotle gave Alexander a copy of Homer's *Iliad*. Reading it, Alexander was supposedly profoundly inspired by the Greek heroes of the Trojan War. He reportedly carried his *Iliad* with him in a special gold box on his military campaigns, keeping the poem and his dagger under his pillow at night.[6]

It is also claimed that during his campaigns in distant lands Alexander sent animal specimens to Aristotle. Supposedly his soldiers, and hunters and fishermen collected creatures for the philosopher. There may be truth to this as some animals Aristotle studied did not live in Greece.

At age fifteen or sixteen, Alexander was appointed regent of Macedon. As regent, he was

Aristotle tutors an adolescent Alexander the Great.

the acting king while Philip was off in battle. Aristotle's tutoring stopped around this time.

King Philip II had several wives after Olympias. Alexander was eighteen years old when his father married for the seventh time. Just after the wedding, Philip was assassinated. Alexander, rather than any of his other children, was presumed to be Philip's heir because of his mother's royal blood. Circumstances were suspicious, but no one knows for sure whether Olympias had a hand in the murder. With Philip's death, Alexander inherited his father's throne. With his political and military skill he was soon on his way to building his vast empire.

5

THE LYCEUM

PLATO'S DEATH IN 347 B.C. MARKED THE end of Aristotle's first period in Athens. Philip of Macedon's death twelve years later marked Aristotle's return to that magnificent city. Athens had fallen under Macedonian control. The year that Aristotle returned to Athens, 335 B.C., Alexander crushed a revolt in the Greek city of Thebes. The Thebans had voted in their democratic assembly to remain independent. The violence and devastation of Alexander's attack was an example to those who resisted him.[1] From Thebes, Alexander, with his boundless ambition, was off on military campaigns to conquer lands to the east.

When Aristotle returned to Athens in 335 B.C., he was about fifty-one years old. He had been a young man just starting his study of philosophy on his first arrival in Athens. This time, he was an experienced philosopher, teacher, and researcher. Married and with a young daughter, Aristotle was quite a wealthy man. His wealth may have been from his family, his wife's family, his Macedonian connections, or a combination of these. He also had colleagues, fellow philosophers including Theophrastus from Lesbos, working with him.

In Athens, the Academy was thriving. Xenocrates, a colleague of Aristotle, had become its director. Aristotle did not return to the Academy. Instead he established a new school. As a metic, a foreign born resident of Athens, Aristotle was not allowed to own property in Athens, so he may have rented the premises for his school.

Aristotle's school made its home in a park-like site known for its lovely groves of plane trees. The area was dedicated to the god Apollo Lycius, Apollo of the Wolves. According to Greek myths, Apollo had once protected Athens from an infestation of hungry wolves. This sanctuary with a gymnasium was established to thank him.[2] Aristotle's school became known as the Lyceum.

The Lyceum was sometimes called the Peripatetic School. Scholars there were known as Peripatetics. The Greek word *peripateo* means to walk around. This unusual title may have come from Aristotle's and other philosophers' habit of walking as they taught. Another explanation for the name is that there was a covered walkway on the grounds, a *peripatos* in Greek. The scholars and students may have gathered in its shade for their teaching.[3]

There were certainly similarities between Aristotle's Lyceum and Plato's Academy. At both, philosophers were teaching younger students. Moral behavior, political theory, and the search for truth were ongoing subjects of interest.

In one important way, the Lyceum was very different from the Academy. Beyond being a center for teaching, the Lyceum was a center for research. This was a place where scholars collected information and investigated many

The stone structures on this site in downtown Athens were recently identified by archaeologists as ruins of Aristotle's Lyceum.

subjects in depth and in an organized way. No earlier school did anything comparable. As the first of its kind, the Lyceum laid the groundwork for later centers like the famous Museum and Library in Alexandria, Egypt.[4] Learning through research was unlike the approach at the Academy. At the Academy, scholars looked to their powers of reasoning to find answers.

Lyceum scholars used reasoning as well, but they also used books, maps, plants, rocks, animal specimens, and other objects in their study. To study politics, for example, the Peripatetics collected the constitutions of 158 cities.[5] With these documents they could read what was similar and different in the communities. They could look at the cities' histories to see if the cities enjoyed peace or were often in wars, if the people prospered or were poor.

The Lyceum was home to one of the world's first important libraries. Reading and writing was widespread in Greece by this time. Plays, poems, government edicts, philosophers' ideas and more were written. This was centuries before the printing press made mass production of books possible. Instead, Greeks had scribes, probably slaves, who copied manuscripts by hand. Books were written on long papyrus scrolls. Papyrus was a type of paper made from reeds that grew in Egypt. By Aristotle's time, there were booksellers in Athens' agora selling scrolls of popular works.[6]

In the Lyceum library, Aristotle would have had copies of Plato's writing. He also must have had works from some of the earliest Greek philosophers like Thales of Miletus. In Aristotle's writing, he sometimes laid out the history of different ideas. For example, in *On the Heavens,* he wrote about earlier Greek theories about Earth's shape and its surroundings. "Anaximenes and Anaxagoras and Democritus give the flatness of the earth as the cause of its staying still. Thus, they say, it does not cut, but covers like a lid, the air beneath it." (294b 15). Because the writings of these earlier thinkers have not survived the centuries, Aristotle's comments about them are among our best sources of information about their thoughts. By offering this background, Aristotle has served as a historian of science.

Besides books and the constitutions, the Lyceum library had maps and a collection of anatomical diagrams.[7] These diagrams would have shown the structure of plants and animals—perhaps the heart, lungs, and other internal organs of an ox, or the skeleton of a horse.

Aristotle and other thinkers at the Lyceum used an empirical approach to much of their research. *Empirical* is sometimes defined as pertaining to or founded upon experiment or experience. We use our senses to make empirical observations. Aristotle especially used his sense of sight to observe animals and then to write detailed descriptions of his observations. Empirical observation is essential to scientific method.

Besides Aristotle, other scholars at the Lyceum did research projects. Some were conducted while Aristotle was there, others in later years. Theophrastus did extensive work on botany, the study of plants. He also wrote "On Stones." Meno wrote a history of Greek medicine. Strato wrote about levers, pulleys, and other simple tools.[8]

In a way the Lyceum was a rival school to Plato's Academy. Some students studied from philosophers at both places. Eratosthenes, who later measured Earth's circumference and was head librarian in Alexandria, was a student of Peripatetics as well as of the Academy.

Sometime after Aristotle founded the Lyceum, his wife died. Aristotle later lived with another woman named Herpyllis. They had a son who they named Nicomachus, like Aristotle's father. One of Aristotle's books is titled *Nicomachean Ethics,* for his son, father, or both. It is also possible that the book was edited by or even written by Aristotle's son.

It is likely that Aristotle did considerable writing while at the Lyceum. It is also possible that he edited and further developed some of his earlier works during this time. Certainly the Lyceum years were very productive for Aristotle.

6

LIVING THINGS

BEFORE ARISTOTLE, THE STUDY OF LIVING things was not a regular part of philosophy. Many Greek philosophers had theories about the heavens and about the substances of Earth, like water and air. Plato theorized about abstract and eternal Forms. Aristotle believed that earthly things, like animals and plants, were worthy of study, too.

Aristotle did a tremendous amount of research and writing about animals. *History of Animals, Parts of Animals, Movement of Animals, Progression of Animals,* and *Generation of Animals* are titles of five of his existing works. For his groundbreaking achievements, he is considered the Father of Life Sciences and the Father of Zoology. Zoology is the branch of biology that deals with animals, their growth, structure, and classification. Aristotle greatly advanced factual knowledge of animals. Altogether, 560 different animal species are mentioned in his writing.[1] These include 120 kinds of fish and 60 kinds of insects.[2] Aristotle was the first thinker to make an organized, science-minded effort to observe and gather information about animals. He not only wrote detailed observations about them, he conducted systematic dissections to understand their anatomy. Aristotle related his knowledge of animals to human beings. Among his inquiries, he tried to understand heredity and repro-duction. He developed theories to explain why animals have their unique characteristics.

In *Parts of Animals*, Aristotle laid out his case for the study of living things:

> Of substances constituted by nature some are ungenerated, imperishable, and eternal, while others are subject to generation and decay. The former are excellent and divine, but less accessible to knowledge. The evidence that might throw light on them, and

on the problems which we long to solve respecting them, is furnished but scantily by sensation, whereas respecting perishable plants and animals we have abundant information, living as we do in their midst, and ample data may be collected concerning all their various kinds, if only we are willing to take sufficient pains. Both departments, however have their special charm. (644b 22-25)

The first substances Aristotle was referring to were the heavens—the stars, planets, sun, and moon. Studying these distant objects was challenging. Greeks could see the stars and use their reasoning powers to try to understand them. There was little information they could collect about them. Before the invention of the telescope, only light and motion of the stars and planets could be observed. Even today, as astronomers and physicists turn high-powered technology to nebulae, black holes, and distant galaxies, the heavens are less accessible to study than things here on Earth.

Aristotle's substances "subject to generation and decay," were those that live, reproduce, and die—living things. We can gather information about plants and animals, he explained, and give them more thorough examination. "In certitude and in completeness our knowledge of terrestrial things has the advantage," he wrote. (645a 2)

Aristotle aimed to deal with all known animals, "without omitting, to the best of our ability, any member of the kingdom, no matter how ignoble." (645a 7) He warned that we should not, "recoil with childish aversion from the examination of the humbler animals. Every realm of nature is marvelous." (645a 15)

History of Animals

Aristotle's *History of Animals* is like an encyclopedia packed full of descriptions. Horses, elephants, crocodiles, ants, snakes, dogfish, lobsters, twelve kinds of bees, spiders, men, wolves, pigeons, lice, deer, sponges, dolphins, and whales are just a few of the creatures he discussed. Of the many animals he studied, 555 are included in this book. In it, he dashed through the animal kingdom, describing creatures and looking at differences and similarities between them. His descriptions are straightforward. For example, the entry on the lobster begins:

> The lobster is all over grey-colored, with a mottling of black. Its under feet, up to the big feet, are eight in number; then come the big feet, far larger and flatter at the tips than the same organs in the crayfish; and these are irregular: the right claw has the extreme flat surface long and thin, while the left claw has the corresponding surface thick and round. Each of the two claws divided at the end like a pair of jaws, has both below and above a set of teeth: only that in the right claw they are small and saw shaped, while in the left claw those at the apex are saw-shaped and those within are molar shaped . . . (526a 13-21)

Aristotle's words accurately describe the type of lobster that lives in the Mediterranean Sea. Clearly, he had carefully and thoroughly examined lobsters. While describing a lobster may not seem very remarkable to us today, before Aristotle, no one had taken this approach to the natural world. His written description could be used to compare the lobster to other creatures. It could also be understood by people who had never seen a lobster. Many sea creatures are described. Much of Aristotle's marine research may date to his months on Lesbos.

In collecting information about animals, Aristotle conducted dissections. Dissection is to cut apart a body in order to examine its parts. He is considered the first thinker to bring this investigative process to the study of nature. Aristotle looked at and described animal hearts, lungs, brains, stomachs, and other organs. He learned about different types of tissues—bone, muscle, cartilage and more. He tried to make sense of the functioning of different organs and tissues. Aristotle dissected animals but not human bodies. His understanding of the inside of the human body was based on his animal studies.

One fascinating description in *History of Animals* is Aristotle's study of the development of a chick inside an egg. Three days after the egg is laid, he noted, there was the first indication of the embryo as a speck of blood in the egg white. It "beats and moves as though endowed with life," he wrote. Veins grow next, then "a little afterwards the body is differentiated. The head is clearly distinguished, and in it the eyes." Aristotle recognized that as the chick was developing in the egg white, it was getting its nourishment from the yolk. At ten days old, "the chick and all its parts are distinctly visible." "About the twentieth day, if you open the egg and touch the chick, it moves inside and chirps; and it is already coming to be covered with down." "After the twentieth day is past, the chick begins to break the shell." The baby bird then emerges into the outside world. (561a 5-30)

Aristotle's study of animals is not without flaws, and sometimes his observations misled him. Eels posed a problem to Aristotle. He never found eel eggs either through dissections or in

ARISTOTELIS:DE HISTORIA:ANIMALIVM: LIBER PRIMVS INTERPRETE THEODORO

NIMALIVM PARTES:AVT IN
cõpositę sũt q̃.f.ĩ similes sibi ptes diuidũt
ut caro ĩ carnes:& ob eã rē similares appellē
tur:aut cõpositę q̃ aptę secari ĩ ptes dissimi
les sint:nõ ĩ similes: ut manus nõ in manus
secaf : aut facies in facies : Quapropter eas
dissimilares noiemus:quo ĩ genere ptiũ sũt:q̃ nõ mõ ptes:ue
rũ etiã mēbra appellēf: uidelicet q̃ cũ ipsę totius itegritate de
scribāf:babeāt tamē intra se ptes diuersas: suiꝗ generis opifi
cia: ut caput:ut pes:ut manus: ut totũ brachium : aut pectus:
Quippe q̃:& ipsa ptes sint totę: & ex ptibus cõstēt diuersis :
Queꝗ aũt ps dissimilaris ex similaribus cõstat: ut manus ex
carne ossibus neruis. babēt uero aĩalia ptes:aut easdē sibi oēs
aut diuersas:partes easdē:uel specie intelligi uolo:ut bominis
nasus:aut oculus specie cũ naso:aut oculo bois alterius cõue
nit:et caro cũ carne:et os cũ osse:Quod idē de equo & cęteris
q̃ specie iter se cõsentire statuimus:ĩtelligi debet:ut.n.totũ se
babet ad totũ: Sic ptes singulę sese ad sigulas babeāt: necesse
ẽuel genere q̃q̃ excessu defectuue iter se differāt:de iis loquor
quorũ idē ē genus:uerbi gratia auis:aut piscis.id.n.utrũꝗ dif
ferētiis cõsumif generis:Et species cõplures:tũ pisciũ: tũ etiã
auiũ babēf:differũt uero iter se ptes pene plurimę eorũ cõtra
ria affectuũ qualitate:ut coloris: aut figurę: eo ꝙ alię magis :
alię minus affectę iis ipsis qualitatibus sint multitudine etiã
& paucitate & magnitudine: puitateꝗ:& oĩno excessu: defe
ctuꝗ discrepant cũ aliis crusta:aliis testa ꝑ tegmine babeatur
& aliis rostrum porrectius sit: ut gruibus : aliis breue:penna
item aliis uberius :aliis partius:data ēſt ſed tamen in bis quo
que ratio partium nonnullarum diuersa ēſt :Cum alia calcari
aut aliquo armentur aculeo : alia nibil eiusmodi babeant: &
aliis apex in capite sit : aliis desit : sed enim quod prope dixe
rim partes plurimę:& ex quibus tota moles compacta ēſt:aut

A page from *De animalibus*, which used Aristotle's *History of Animals* as its main source.

78

the places they lived. He noted that other writers claimed to have seen "worms" (maybe baby eels) inside eels, but Aristotle thought they were wrong. He concluded that "eels are derived from the so-called 'earth's guts' that grow spontaneously in mud and in humid ground." (570a 4–15). It is understandable that eels confounded Aristotle. The eels that he saw in Greek waters spawn in the Atlantic Ocean. They are born in the ocean, then journey for about three years to rivers and lakes. They return to the ocean to have their young. Eel spawning was not observed and documented until the 1920s.[3]

History of Animals was one of the major works in this field in the ancient world. In the centuries after Aristotle, it was translated into Arabic and Latin. In the European Renaissance it was the main source of the leading zoology book, *De animalibus,* into the sixteenth century.[4]

Parts of Animals

Aristotle's *Parts of Animals* examined physiology and presented Aristotle's explanations of why animals have their bodies. Physiology is the branch of biology that deals with the internal workings of living things. This text looks at how bodies serve the purposes of different specific creatures.

In human and animal bodies, Aristotle proposes, "there are three different degrees of composition; and of these the first in order, as all will allow is composition of what some call the elements, such as earth air, water, fire." (646a 12-16) Today, our understanding of chemical elements is different from the Greeks' four elements. However, his assessment is similar to our understanding that the human body is made up of chemical elements including hydrogen, oxygen, and carbon. "The second degree of composition is that by which the homogeneous parts of animals, such as bone, flesh, and the like, are constituted out of the primary substances." (646a 21-24) We now know these as tissues—muscle, nerve, bone, cartilage, and more. "The third and last stage is the composition which forms the heterogeneous parts, such as the face, hand, and the rest." (646a 28)

Aristotle explored these compositions. Regarding tissues and organs, like blood and brains, he suggested their purposes. "The ribs, for example, which enclose the chest are intended to ensure the safety of the heart and neighboring viscera," he wrote. (655a 1-2) The heart, liver, kidneys, stomach, esophagus, lungs, and gallbladder were described. He discussed these organs in animals and also their workings in the human body.

"Nature never makes anything superfluous," Aristotle held. (691b 4-5) In other words, hearts, brains, legs, arms, teeth, jaws, and other parts are suited for the animal's needs. As an example, he explained that crocodiles snap with their upper jaws rather than their lower ones. On most animals, it is the lower jaw that moves. In crocodiles, though, Aristotle said, this is reversed, "because the feet in this creature are so excessively small as to be useless for seizing and holding prey; on which account nature has given it a mouth that can serve for these purposes in their stead." (691b 5-11) Aristotle offers many examples of parts of animals serving the appropriate function of that animal's life and environment.

"In birds the mouth consists of what is called the beak, which in them is a substitute for lips and teeth. This beak presents variations in harmony with the functions and protective purposes which it serves," wrote Aristotle. (662b 1) In meat-eating birds, he noted, the beak is hooked and "suited for deeds of violence." He is correct—eagles, hawks and other birds that eat small animals and fish have sharp hooked beaks that are strong enough to tear flesh. "Similarly in each other kind of bird the beak is suited to the mode of life." He wrote, "In woodpeckers it is hard and strong . . . in the smaller birds it is delicate, so as to be of use in collecting seeds and picking up minute animals." Aristotle saw each animal as suited to its habitat.

In the 1800s, another student of nature also made observations of birds' beaks. On a voyage in the Pacific Ocean, Charles Darwin collected birds from different Galapagos Islands. Darwin

A. Woodpecker Finch   D. Mangrove Finch

B. Warbler Finch   E. Small Ground Finch

C. Cactus Finch   F. Medium Ground Finch

Darwin's theory of natural selection explains why the beaks of finches from different Galapagos Islands looked different. The birds' beaks adapted to the specific food sources found on each island. Hundreds of years before Darwin, Aristotle had made similar observations on the various structures and functions of birds' beaks.

saw that the bodies of the finches from different islands were the same, but their beaks were different. Different plants grew on different islands. Darwin saw that the birds' beaks were appropriate for eating different kinds of seeds. He used this observation and others in setting forth his theory of evolution of species. His theory is called natural selection. According to Darwin, birds with beaks suitable to the food on their island would be the ones who survived and reproduced. Through this survival process, different species evolved.

Aristotle was not an evolutionist. He did not believe that creatures evolved over time. Instead, he saw that there were causes for all things in nature. Among the causes, Aristotle believed that each living thing had a "final cause" within itself. The final cause was what it was for, its purpose, in Aristotle's words "that for the sake of which" a thing exists. (194a 36)

7

CAUSES AND LOGIC

ARISTOTLE BELIEVED THAT IT WAS HUMAN nature to seek knowledge and that knowledge was different from opinions. "Knowledge is the object of our inquiry, and men do not think they know a thing till they have grasped the "why" of it," he wrote in his book *Physics*. (194b 18-20) *Physics* examined motion and change. Knowledge was not just saying that something was true, believed Aristotle, but knowing the causes and principles that made it true. Aristotle did not just want to know that the sun would rise and set day after day, he wanted to know why. He wanted to know why birds had different beaks, why oceans did not overflow, and why planets moved unevenly through the night sky.

Beyond wondering about an almost endless list of subjects, Aristotle gave a great deal of thought to finding satisfactory answers to "why." He set out methods for inquiring into nature. He then presented his answers in an organized way. *Physics* shows this approach. "Nature is a principle of motion and change, and it is the subject of our inquiry," he wrote. (200b 12) It opens:

> When the objects of an inquiry, in any department, have principles, causes, or elements, it is through acquaintance with these that knowledge and understanding is attained. For we do not think we know a thing until we are acquainted with its primary causes or first principles, and have carried our analysis as far as its elements. Plainly therefore, in the science of nature too our first task will be to try to determine what relates to its principles.
>
> The natural way of doing this is to start from the things which are more knowable and clear to us and proceed toward those which are

clearer and more knowable by nature . . . Thus we must advance from universals to particulars; for it is a whole that is more knowable to sense-perception . . . Similarly a child begins by calling all men father, and all women mother, but later on distinguishes each of them. (184a 10–184b 13)

After stating his goal, Aristotle sometimes examined what others had said about the subject he would examine. He agreed with and built upon certain ideas. For others, he showed how they were flawed. After examining other theories, Aristotle presented his own theories. He built his arguments using reasoning and evidence. His structure is still used in writing research papers today.

Four Causes

In Aristotle's science, he was trying to under-stand the world he saw and experienced. It was a world of physical objects and ongoing change. In trying to explain the world, he needed to address change. For example, a little acorn could grow into a huge oak tree—an object very different than the acorn. The tree could then be cut down and made into furniture. Silver could be mined from the ground, then made into a bowl by a craftsman.

Aristotle believed that in order to have knowledge of a thing, we must know the four causes that made it so. An answer was not complete and adequate unless it addressed all four causes.[1] These four causes are central to Aristotle's philosophy. They are mentioned in many of his texts and explained in detail in *Physics*.

Aristotle's four causes were: the material cause, the formal cause, the efficient cause, and the final cause. The material cause was the matter of which a thing was made. The formal cause was the shape or structure of it. The efficient cause was what brought it into being. The final cause was what it was for, its purpose.[2]

An example can help us understand Aristotle's causes. Imagine seeing a marble statue of George Washington in a park. The material cause of the statue is the marble, the matter from which it is made. The formal cause is the shape of George Washington. The statue is not actually George Washington, but it is formed like him. The statue is in his shape. The efficient cause is the artist who made the statue—the sculptor who chiseled it from the block of marble. What then is the final cause of the statue? Why was it made and put in this park? The statue's final cause is to honor George Washington's contributions as a founding father of the United States. The final cause is the reason why it exists.

Looking at nature, we can consider Aristotle's view of the causes of a horse. The material cause of a horse, according to Aristotle, was its mother. In reproduction, he thought the female alone provided the matter for the baby. The form was what makes horses different from other animals. The formal cause was becoming a four-legged creature with a mane, that gallops, and can carry a rider or pull a chariot. According to Aristotle, the father supplied the moving cause as his part in reproduction. The final cause would be the perfect, full grown adult horse.[3]

Aristotle did not suggest that nature had a conscious purpose. He did think though that there were "ends" in nature. Horses gave birth to horses, wheat grew from wheat seeds, a boy grew to be a man. Aristotle believed that living things had "final causes" within themselves.[4]

> It is clear then that there are causes, and the number of them is what we have stated [four]. The number is the same as that of the things comprehended under the question 'why.' The 'why' is referred ultimately either, in things which do not involve motion, e.g. in mathematics, to the 'what' (to the definition of a straight line . . . or the like); or to what initiated a motion, e.g. 'why did they go to war?—because there had been a raid'; or we are inquiring 'for the sake of what'—'that they may rule': or in the case of things that come, we are looking for the matter . . .

> Now, the causes being four, it is the business of the student of nature to know about them all,

and if he refers his problems back to all of them, he will assign the 'why' in the proper way to do his science—the matter, the form, the mover, that for the sake of which. (198a 7-25)

The search for causes occurs throughout Aristotle's writing. Often the line between different causes is unclear to us. In following Aristotle's thinking, we see that his search for causes guided his investigations.

Logic

Five of Aristotle's existing works are usually grouped together under the title of the *Organon*. *Organon* means "instrument" or "tool." Aristotle did not put these works together himself, nor did he use the title *Organon*. The name and grouping came after his time. These works lay out rules of logic and argumentation for investigations. Aristotle is considered the "Father of Logic."

Logic comes from the ancient Greek word *logos,* meaning "the word." Logic is the study of the principles of reasoning. It applies in thinking, speaking, and writing. Logical arguments build one idea or fact on another. Aristotle's logic is centered on deductive reasoning. Deductive reasoning means moving from a general idea to a specific one. The Greek word *sullogismos* means "deductive argument." What is now known as a "syllogism" is the structure that Aristotle described.

Examples of syllogisms demonstrate this tool of reasoning:

> All humans are mortal,
>
> All Greeks are humans,
>
> All Greeks are mortal.

Another syllogism in the same form is:

> All birds have feathers.
>
> All parakeets are birds,
>
> All parakeets have feathers.

In each of these examples, we can see that we began with two sentences that could be accepted as truth. These sentences are called premises. From these two true statements, we can conclude a third sentence, different from the premises, but that is necessarily true. Together, these three could be called a valid argument. Aristotle showed how different statements are used in syllogisms.

When Aristotle explained syllogisms, he was clear that these rules could be applied to many subjects. He did not use specific sentences to show how they worked—he used letters of the alphabet. Discussing universal negative terms, for example, he wrote, "First let us take a universal negative with the terms A and B. Now if A belongs to no B, B will not belong to any A; for if it does belong to some B (say to C) it will not be true that A belongs to no B—for C is one of the Bs." (25a 14-16)

Aristotle identified different kinds of premises that could be used in syllogisms. Some statements are universal: all cats are animals. Universal statements can also be negative: no cats are fish. Some statements are particular: this cat is black. Some are indefinite: some cats are black. With different types of statements, Aristotle identified forty-eight different kinds of syllogisms. Of these, he showed that fourteen presented valid arguments.

Aristotle presented other tools besides syllogism in the *Organon*. He looked at reasoning, argument and language.[5] He examined how to demonstrate that something was true. His demonstrations are in some ways similar to developments in ancient Greek mathematics. In mathematics, especially geometry, Greeks laid out "proofs." For example, they did not just state the relationship between the length of sides of a right triangle. They showed steps that stated a series of truths, that when taken together proved a relationship in all right triangles.

Aristotle's development of logic is really a remarkable achievement. People had used syllogisms in their thinking and writing before him. Aristotle, though, recognized and explained how statements could work together to prove knowledge.

ELEMENTS AND THE UNIVERSE

AS ARISTOTLE AND GREEK PHILOSOPHERS sought knowledge, they moved away from supernatural explanations for natural phenomena. Aristotle gathered observations and did research. He used his reasoning to try to find causes. In investigating different subjects, he examined opinions of other philosophers. He also used his logic to prove his theories.

In his studies, Aristotle tackled two especially perplexing problems. Concerned with the physical world, Aristotle wanted to know what it was made of—its matter. Aristotle also wanted to know where we are in the universe.

Four Elements

Aristotle was not the only ancient thinker who tried to understand the physical matter of the world. Thales of Miletus, one of the very first Greek philosophers, lived in the sixth century B.C. Thales suggested that water was the world's fundamental matter. Anaximander did not suggest a specific substance. He believed that something indefinite made up the world. He called it the Boundless.[1] Philosophers known as Atomists proposed that matter was made up of tiny particles. The particles were called atoms, which means indivisible. The atoms were infinite and constantly moving. Different combinations of atoms formed different kinds of matter.[2] The Atomists' ideas differ from our modern under-standing of atoms and molecules, but this was a remarkable theory.

Empedocles, who lived about a century before Aristotle, suggested that there were four basic elements: earth, air, fire, and water. He believed that these separated and combined into different substances. Empedocles identified forces that influenced the elements. He called these forces Love and Strife. Love drew things together. Strife tore them apart.[3]

Aristotle accepted and built upon some of Empedocles' ideas. He carried the theory further, identifying four qualities that affected the elements. Using examples of real substances and observed changes he showed how his understanding of matter was plausible.

Aristotle accepted Empedocles' four elements—earth, water, air, and fire. We can see that these relate to states of matter. Earth is a solid. Water is liquid. Air is gas. Fire we now know is a process called combustion.[4] For Aristotle, each element had a natural movement. Fire and air moved upward. Earth and water moved down. Now we identify this downward attraction to the earth as gravity.

Four different qualities acted on Aristotle's elements. These qualities were opposite pairs: hot and cold, wet and dry. Each element consisted of a pair of qualities. Water was cold and wet. Earth was cold and dry. Fire was hot and dry. Air was hot and wet. Changes could take place in the elements. Water, for example could change from cold and wet by being boiled or through evaporation. Through these processes, Aristotle said, it changed to "air"—actually water vapor. Air (hot and wet) could change back to water—falling as rain or condensing on a cold surface.[5]

Some of Aristotle's discussions of water and the water cycle are quite far-sighted. In *Meteorology* he wrote about the sea: "All rivers and all the water that is generated flow into it; for water flows into the deepest place, and the deepest part of the earth is filled by the sea. But part of it is all quickly carried up by the sun, while the rest remains." With rivers constantly flowing into it, why did the sea not overflow? Aristotle explained, "The solution is easy. The same amount of water does not take as long to dry up as when it is spread out as when it is gathered in a body." (355b 16-26) Over the vast surface area of the ocean, evaporation was happening steadily. Water was constantly returning to air. The water would fall again as rain and be carried by rivers back to the sea.

Aristotle knew the world's substances were not just pure examples of the four elements. He

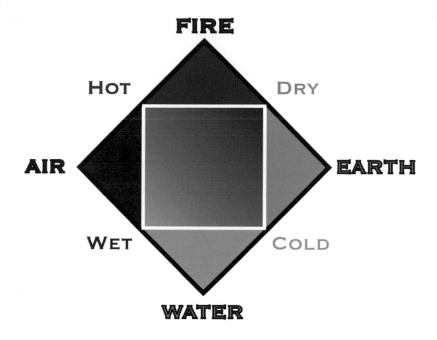

Aristotle believed that substances were made of combinations of four elements: fire, air, earth, and water.

examined compounds, matter made of more than one substance. Some of these were chemical compounds—two substances making a different third one. When copper and tin are combined they make bronze, for example, and the copper and tin cannot be separated out again. He noted that some substances keep their original properties and do not change. Barley seeds and wheat seeds could be mixed, but they did not change. After being mixed together, they could be separated and the seeds would still have their original characteristics.[6]

Aristotle looked at the physical properties of many familiar substances. He studied substances that burned, like wood, and those that did not, like stone. He considered those that melt—like wax, silver, and ice. Some substances, like salt, dissolved in water. Some thickened when cold, others hardened when dried. Aristotle's book *Meteorology* shows him using research and observations to understand substances.

Aristotle's ideas of four elements and four qualities can seem quaint to us today. At the same time we see that his theories were based on observations and experiences of substances and nature. We can also appreciate that today we understand substances in terms of different elements—chemical elements. A chemical element is any of the more than one hundred known substances (of which ninety-two occur naturally) that cannot be separated into simpler substances. Singly or in combination, chemical elements constitute all matter.

Earth in the Universe

Considering Aristotle's view of the universe, we start by looking at the information he had available. When ancient Greeks looked at the sky they saw the sun rising and setting in a regular pattern. The moon's movements were more complicated with its 29 ½ day cycle. The stars appeared as twinkling dots of light on a great rotating dome. They did not change position relative to each other. The stars of asterisms like the Big Dipper were reliably in their positions. Five planets—Mercury, Venus, Mars, Jupiter, and Saturn—were known. These can all be seen with the naked eye. Unlike the stars, each planet followed its own separate, sometimes meandering, path. To the Greeks, the planets appeared to wander across the skies. Sometimes, when viewed after night, a planet moved in a steady direction relative to the stars; sometimes it appeared to move backward. The word "planet" comes from the Greek for "wanderer."

Today we can predict the observed movements of the heavenly bodies because of our understanding of the solar system. We now know that the sun is at the center of our system and that the planets, including Earth, revolve around it. The planets' orbits, we know, are not circular but elliptical. We know that moons revolve around some planets. This view of the universe did not take shape until nearly two thousand years after Aristotle.

In writing about the universe. Aristotle started by reviewing what other thinkers said about Earth and its shape and position in the universe. He explored the ideas of Xenophanes and Anaximenes. Xenophanes suggested that Earth beneath us was infinite. Anaximenes thought that Earth was flat, like a lid on air beneath it. Aristotle showed flaws in both of these theories.

Aristotle argued that Earth was a sphere and that it was located in the center of the universe.

In Aristotle's scheme of elements, earth naturally fell down. All earth would necessarily gather like a ball, he thought. He presented evidence of its shape. We see Earth's round shadow when it glides across the face of the moon, he noted. "In eclipses the outline is always curved; and, since it is the interposition of the earth that makes the eclipse, the form of this line will be caused by the form of the earth's surface, which is therefore spherical." (297b 26-30) He also observed that when we travel north or south we see the stars in different positions above the horizon. "Our observations of the stars make it evident, not only that the earth is circular, but also that it is a circle of no great size. There is much change I mean, in the stars which are overhead . . . as one moves northward of southward. Indeed there are some stars seen in Egypt . . . which are not seen in the northerly regions; and stars, which in the north are never beyond the range of observation, in those regions rise and set. All of which goes to show not only that it is a sphere, but of no great size; for otherwise the effect of so slight a change of place would not be so quickly apparent." (297b 30–298a 8)

Explaining the movements of the heavens, Aristotle built on the theories of Eudoxus. Eudoxus was a mathematician at Plato's Academy. Eudoxus believed that movements of heavenly bodies could be explained by a system of nested celestial spheres, turning around Earth. Aristotle agreed that the heavens rather than Earth must be moving. He argued that if Earth was rotating, as some thinkers suggested, we would feel its movement.

A problem for Aristotle was the material moving in the universe. The four elements each had their own natural motion. Clearly the movement of the heavens was different. Aristotle did not believe that the heavens could have empty space between the planets and stars. He did not think it was possible for there to be nothing, what we today call a vacuum. The heavens, therefore, must be made of some special material. Aristotle decided that the heavens must be composed of a fifth element. He called this element "aether."

The aether included a system of concentric spheres for the heavenly bodies. Its natural movement was circular.

The mover of this system, Aristotle wrote, "moves without being moved, being eternal, substance, and actuality." (1072a 26) He called it the "unmoved mover," and saw it as a final cause. Aristotle also wrote about God and goodness in this section of *Metaphysics*. His "unmoved mover" is often seen as his idea of God.

Adding aether and an "unmoved mover" to Eudoxus's plan still did not make it possible to predict the movements of the planets. Aristotle suggested that there were even more spheres. These heavenly spheres had different tilts to their axes and turned at different speeds. Altogether his system included 55 different spheres.[7]

Aristotle's model looks different from our understanding of the solar system. However, with thought, we see that he found answers using his framework of matter. He presented his argument rationally. Aristotle's plan of the universe was refined about five hundred years later by a Greek thinker named Claudius Ptolemy. Ptolemy kept some of Aristotle's spheres and perfect circular motion. He added little spheres to the big ones to help explain the planets' movements.

Aristotle's and Ptolemy's combined system was not seriously challenged until the 1500s. People then saw that Ptolemy's charts of the planets' movements were not accurate. (Accuracy was important partly because many people believed in astrology—that the movements of the heavens influenced people's lives.) Nicolaus Copernicus wrote a book suggesting that observed heavenly movements could be explained by a Sun-centered (rather than Earth-centered) system. A few years later, Galileo Galilee turned his telescope (one of the first) to the heavens and saw moons revolving around the planet Jupiter. Aristotle's spheres and aether gradually gave way to a new understanding of the solar system.

9

THE WORLD AFTER ARISTOTLE

ON JUNE 10, 323 B.C., ALEXANDER THE Great died in Babylon. He had been planning another major military campaign of conquest. There were rumors that he was poisoned, but it is likely that he succumbed to infection. Alexander was not quite thirty-three years old. With his death, there was no clear successor to his empire.

Aristotle was in Athens, still at the Lyceum, when Alexander perished. While Aristotle may have mourned his former student's death, Athenians did not. With Alexander gone, anti-Macedonian feeling erupted. This powerful and brutal leader no longer controlled their city. Aristotle soon left Athens.

History and archaeology have passed on a few tidbits about Aristotle's decision to leave. One account says that he left because he was charged with impiety. Impiety was lack of respect for the gods. Impiety was one of the charges leveled against Socrates. An eloquent poem written by Aristotle about his father-in-law, Hermias, was supposedly the cause for this accusation. The poem still exists. In it, Aristotle compared Hermias to Greek gods.[1] This may have offended some Athenians as Hermias had been born a slave.

A second account of Aristotle's departure reports that he left because he was stripped of honors that had been given to him. Recently, archaeologists found an inscribed stone in Delphi, the most important religious center in ancient Greece. The discovery may support this version of Aristotle's departure. The inscription "praised and crowned" Aristotle.[2] The inscription was found broken at the bottom of a well. In anger against Macedon or possibly against Aristotle himself, the Athenians may have removed the award from its prominent place in Delphi and thrown it down the well.

This stone is supposedly inscribed with a dedication to Aristotle by his former student Alexander the Great. Aristotle had numerous honors granted to him. However, not all Athenians believed he deserved them, which may be one reason Aristotle left Athens.

From Athens, Aristotle moved to the island of Euboea. His mother's family had land there. Aristotle apparently owned houses there and in Stagira. Aristotle died within a year of leaving Athens. He was about sixty-two years old.

We get our final glimpse of Aristotle through his will as passed on by the biographer Diogenes Laertius. "All will be well, but in case anything should happen, Aristotle has made these dispositions," he wrote.[3] A Macedonian, Antipater, was to handle the details of his property. He asked that Theophrastus and others take care of his children and Herpyllis. He left to Herpyllis three maids, a manservant, some silver, and a choice of a house in Euboea or in Stagira. He freed several of his slaves. He arranged for his daughter's servants to be freed and given money when she married. Aristotle specified that several statues be made for temples to honor his mother and certain friends. These included life-size stone statues dedicated to Zeus and Athena for his hometown of Stagira. Aristotle asked that the bones of his wife Pythias be buried with him.[4]

Neither the Lyceum, nor Aristotle's library and writings, are mentioned in his will. Theophrastus became the school's next director. Research projects and teaching continued there through his years and beyond.

Aristotle's writing did not all survive the ancient world. A list from the second century B.C. includes about 150 books—today we have about a fifth of them. Books were copied by hand then. As papyrus grew brittle or rotted, works were sometimes lost forever. Some of Aristotle's writing may have gone to the great library in Alexandria, Egypt. The Alexandrian Library was founded about forty years after Aristotle's death. Islamic scholars in the House of Wisdom in Baghdad had some of Aristotle's works in the 800s A.D. These were translated into Arabic and studied. Byzantine scholars also studied Aristotle. In the 1200s A.D., Aristotle's writing was rediscovered by Europeans. His works were translated into Latin, the language of education at the time. Thomas Aquinas, a Dominican monk, was influential in reconciling Aristotle's

Italian philosopher and theologian Thomas Aquinas (c. 1225–1274), who combined Aristotle's ideas with Christian beliefs. He held the view that reason and faith did not contradict each other.

views with the views of Christianity. Reason and faith could go together, he argued. University students in Paris in 1255 were studying Aristotle.[5]

With the invention of the moveable type printing press in the mid-1400s, literacy raced through Europe. Aristotle's ideas were available to new generations of thinkers. As he had questioned the theories of earlier philosophers, new scientists questioned his views. Besides books, by the 1600s they had new tools—telescopes, microscopes, clocks, even machines that could remove air and create a vacuum. With these instruments and their powers of reason, thinkers suggested theories and used their observations to prove new knowledge. Copernicus, Galileo, and Kepler explained the order of the solar system. Robert Boyle showed that contrary to Aristotle's view, a vacuum could exist—there could be nothing in space. Isaac Newton used mathematics and observations to prove three laws of motion, at last explaining planetary movement. Chemists, biologists, and physicists tackled questions about matter, life, and forces and found new answers.

In the modern world, we do not turn to Aristotle for facts about the elements or the movements of the heavens. Our knowledge of the world, though, was shaped with the influence of his great contributions to science. He advanced factual knowledge in zoology and botany. He laid out basic questions that centuries of thinkers would explore. He provided tools for studying and explaining the realities around us. He also showed the value of empirical research—collecting information and observing specimens and phenomena in a systematic, organized way.[6] We can still turn to Aristotle to learn how to think, to structure logical arguments, and to wonder. "All men by nature desire to know," he wrote. His writing still guides us to think about strange things we see in everyday life and the bigger puzzles of the world.

ACTIVITIES

Reading Aristotle

There is no better source for learning about Aristotle than Aristotle himself. Most school libraries have books about Aristotle and books with either his complete works or selections of his writings. Many Web sites have Aristotle's texts online.

Aristotle's questions are relevant today and well worth exploring. Although some of his vocabulary and ideas can be confusing, reading Aristotle can be very rewarding. One way to start reading Aristotle is to follow his own order of the development of sciences. Aristotle saw that productive sciences emerged first, then practical sciences, and then theoretical sciences.

Beginning with productive science, you may start by reading some of Aristotle's *Rhetoric* or *Poetics*. Productive sciences, said Aristotle, are produced by people. Rhetoric is persuasive speech or writing. Aristotle explains that, "Rhetoric is useful because things that are true and things that are just have a natural tendency to prevail over their opposites." (1355a 21)

Aristotle's practical science deals with human behavior and actions. *Politics* or *Economics* could be a good starting point. You might also sample some of *Nicomachean Ethics*.

For theoretical sciences, *History of Animals* offers some delightful descriptions. From there, you may want to explore *Metaphysics* or *Physics* and/or go on to other works.

Reading Aristotle, do not get discouraged by references or vocabulary that you do not understand. Aristotle is not learned through a single reading. Give yourself time to savor the thoughts that speak to you. Read, think, and return. As you find ideas in Aristotle that resonate, look in your school or local library for books that can help you learn more about Aristotle's philosophy.

Observation and Description

Among Aristotle's many contributions to the history of science was his approach to research. He gathered information, made observations, and presented his observations and theories in an organized way. His data-gathering is especially evident in *History of Animals*. Aristotle was trying to explain all of reality. In his efforts, he tried to write about all animals.

You can keep a list of animals that you observe over a period of a few days. Include small ones—ants, bees, moths, houseflies—as well as domestic animals like cats and dogs, and wild animals including birds, squirrels, and fish. Even if you live in a city, you will probably be surprised by the diversity of life around you. As you list them, think about and note some of their features that distinguish them from other animals.

You may want to read more of Aristotle's descriptions in *History of Animals* to see how he structured his descriptions and the types of features he noted.

Discoveries and Advances

Aristotle was laying building blocks for science 2,400 years ago. Today, we live in an age of amazing scientific advances. Magazines, newspapers, Web sites, and television programs report scientific breakthroughs and discoveries.

Over about a week's time, pay attention to news sources and make a list of science stories. Some may deal with discoveries in space, or medical advances, or endangered animals. As you read about these contemporary achievements and issues, think about Aristotle's curiosity and how they might relate to his ideas of reality and causes.

CHRONOLOGY

429 B.C.—Plato is born.

399 B.C.—Socrates is convicted of corrupting the youth of Athens and is executed.

384 B.C.—Aristotle is born in Stagira to Nicomachus and Phaestis.

385–380 B.C.—Plato founds the Academy in Athens.

367 B.C.—Aristotle studies at Plato's Academy in Athens.

347 B.C.—Plato dies; Aristotle leaves Athens and lives in Assos, on the coast of Turkey, where he marries Pythias.

346–345 B.C.—Aristotle and Pythias move to Lesbos, where he studies marine animals with Theophrastus.

343 B.C.—Aristotle goes to the court of Philip of Macedon, where he reportedly serves as a tutor to Philip's son Alexander.

336 B.C.—Philip II of Macedon dies, and Alexander inherits his throne and begins building his empire.

335 B.C.—Aristotle returns to Athens and founds the Lyceum.

323 B.C.—Alexander the Great dies; Aristotle leaves Athens for Euboea, where he has a home from his mother's estate.

322 B.C.—Aristotle dies on Euboea.

CHAPTER NOTES

Chapter 1. "Desire to Know"

1. If a reader consults a translation other than the Jonathan Barnes edition of *The Complete Works of Aristotle*, the wording of the quotation may not be exactly what is stated. The idea being communicated, however, will be the same. The Bekker number refers to the line of text in a Greek language edition of Aristotle which is used as the basis for most English translations of the philosopher. Different translators find slightly different meanings in the same words or groups of words.

This list indicates the Bekker numbers of first through last lines of Aristotle's treatises quoted in this book.

Lines	Source
24a 10—70b 38	*Prior Analytics*
184a 10—267b 26	*Physics*
268a 1—313b 23	*On the Heavens*
486a 5—638b 38	*History of Animals*
639a 1—697b 30	*Parts of Animals*
980a 22—1093b 29	*Metaphysics*
1094a 1—1181b 23	*Nicomachean Ethics*
1252a 1—1342b 34	*Politics*
1343a 1—1353b 26	*Economics*

2. T. E. Rihll, *Greek Science* (Oxford: Oxford University Press, 1999), p. 2.

3. Christopher Shields, *Aristotle* (New York: Routledge, 2007), pp. 416–417.

4. Ibid., pp. 31–32.

5. Ibid., p 32.

6. Ibid., p. 29.

7. Ibid., p. 23.

8. Jonathan Barnes, ed., *The Cambridge Companion to Aristotle* (New York: Cambridge University Press, 1995), p. 12.

9. Ibid.

10. Ibid.

11. G. E. R. Lloyd, *Early Greek Science: Thales to Aristotle* (New York: W. W. Norton and Company, 1970), p. 8.

12. Ibid., pp. 144–145.

Chapter 2. The Stagirite

1. M. I. Finley, *The Portable Greek Historians: The Essence of Herodotus, Thucydides, Xenophon, Polybius* (New York: The Viking Press, 1959, 1972 printing), p. 215, (Herodotus 8.144).

2. Paul Cartledge, *Alexander the Great: The Hunt for a New Past* (New York: The Overlook Press, 2004), p. 45.

3. Jonathan Barnes, ed., *The Cambridge Companion to Aristotle* (New York: Cambridge University Press, 1995), p. 3.

Chapter 3. Academy and Athens

1. Jonathan Barnes, ed., *The Cambridge Companion to Aristotle* (New York: Cambridge University Press, 1995), p. 4.

2. John Boardman, ed., *The Oxford History of the Classical World* (Oxford: Oxford University Press, 1986) p. 137.

3. Ibid., p. 229.

4. G. E. R. Lloyd, *Early Greek Science: Thales to Aristotle* (New York: W. W. Norton and Company, 1970), p. 66.

5. Paul Cartledge, ed., *The Cambridge Illustrated History of Ancient Greece* (New York: Cambridge University Press, 1998), p. 300.

6. Catherine B. Avery, ed., *The New Century Classical Handbook* (New York: Appleton-Century-Crofts, 1962), p. 901.

7. Ibid.

8. Edith Hamilton and Huntington Cairns, eds., *The Collected Dialogues of Plato* (Princeton, N.J.: Princeton University Press, 2005), p. 427.

9. Christopher Shields, *Aristotle* (New York: Routledge, 2007), p. 18.

10. G. E. R. Lloyd, *Aristotle: The Growth and Structure of His Thought* (London: Cambridge University Press, 1968), p. 5.

Chapter 4. Assos, Lesbos, and Alexander

1. Edith Hamilton and Huntington Cairns, eds., *The Collected Dialogues of Plato* (Princeton, N.J.: Princeton University Press, 2005), p. 1603.

2. Jonathan Barnes, ed., *The Cambridge Companion to Aristotle* (New York: Cambridge University Press, 1995), p. 5.

3. Felix Grayeff, *Aristotle and His School* (New York: Barnes and Noble, 1974) p. 28.

4. Grayeff, p. 29

5. Diogenes Laertius, *Lives of Eminent Philosophers* (Cambridge, Mass.: Harvard University Press, 1972), vol. 1, p. 447.

6. Paul Cartledge, *Alexander the Great: The Hunt for a New Past* (New York: The Overlook Press, 2004), p. 227.

Chapter 5. The Lyceum

1. Paul Cartledge, *Alexander the Great: The Hunt for a New Past* (New York: The Overlook Press, 2004), p. 111.

2. Catherine B. Avery, ed., *The New Century Classical Handbook* (New York: Appleton-Century-Crofts, 1962), p. 653.

3. Christopher Shields, *Aristotle* (New York: Routledge, 2007), p. 20.

4. G. E. R. Lloyd, *Aristotle: The Growth and Structure of His Thought* (London: Cambridge University Press, 1968), pp. 98–99.

5. Shields, p. 21.

6. Gail Fine, ed., *The Oxford Handbook of Plato* (New York: Oxford University Press, 2008), p. 65.

7. Lloyd, p. 100.

8. Ibid., p. 101.

Chapter 6. Living Things

1. D. M. Balme, "Aristotle: Natural History and Zoology," *Dictionary of Scientific Biography,* p. 259.

2. G. E. R. Lloyd, *Early Greek Science: Thales to Aristotle* (New York: W. W. Norton and Company, 1970), p. 116.

3. T. E. Rihll, *Greek Science* (Oxford: Oxford University Press, 1999), p. 109.

4. Balme, p. 266.

Chapter 7. Causes and Logic

1. Christopher Shields, *Aristotle* (New York: Routledge, 2007), p. 44.

2. Ibid.

3. G. E. R. Lloyd, *Aristotle: The Growth and Structure of His Thought* (London: Cambridge University Press, 1968), p. 60.

4. Ibid., pp. 61–62.

5. Jonathan Barnes, ed., *The Cambridge Companion to Aristotle* (New York: Cambridge University Press, 1995), p. 28.

Chapter 8. Elements and the Universe

1. G. E. R. Lloyd, *Early Greek Science: Thales to Aristotle* (New York: W. W. Norton and Company, 1970), p. 20.

2. Ibid., p. 46.

3. Paul Cartledge, ed., *The Cambridge Illustrated History of Ancient Greece* (NewYork: Cambridge University Press, 1998), p. 297.

4. G. E. R. Lloyd, *Aristotle: The Growth and Structure of His Thought* (London: Cambridge University Press, 1968), p. 166.

5. Ibid., p. 169.

6. Ibid., p. 173.

7. Ibid., pp. 149–53.

Chapter 9. The World After Aristotle

1. Christopher Shields, *Aristotle* (New York: Routledge, 2007), p. 21.

2. Jonathan Barnes, ed., *The Cambridge Companion to Aristotle* (New York: Cambridge University Press, 1995), p. 6.

3. Diogenes Laertius, *Lives of Eminent Philosophers* (Cambridge, Mass.: Harvard University Press, 1972), vol. 1, p. 455.

4. Ibid.

5. G. E. R. Lloyd, *Aristotle: The Growth and Structure of His Thought* (London: Cambridge University Press, 1968), p. 311.

6. G. E. R. Lloyd, *Early Greek Science: Thales to Aristotle* (New York: W. W. Norton and Company, 1970), pp. 144–145.

GLOSSARY

academy—An educational institution or society to promote a particular aspect of culture.

Academy—School founded by Plato.

acropolis—The high ground in an ancient Greek city. Temples were usually built on these prominent sites.

agora—The business and commercial center of a Greek city.

arete—Greek word for virtue or excellence.

Assembly—Meeting of adult male citizens who had decision-making power in a Greek state.

chemical element—Any of the more than one hundred known substances (of which ninety-two occur naturally) that cannot be separated into simpler substances. Singly or in combination, chemical elements constitute all matter.

dialectic—Discussion and reasoning by dialogue as a method of intellectual investigation.

element—To the ancient Greeks, one of four substances thought to constitute the physical universe: fire, air, earth, and water.

empirical—Pertaining to or founded upon experiment or experience.

episteme—Ancient Greek word for knowledge. Aristotle saw episteme as an organized body of knowledge and as the state of knowing. Episteme is the root of "science."

esoteric—Intended for or understood by an informed group of people.

ethics—The study of moral behavior.

exoteric—Capable of being understood by most people, not just an informed group.

gymnasium—A Greek school where young men went for athletic training. Gymnasia were social and intellectual centers.

logic—The study of the principles of reasoning. Aristotle's logic is centered on deductive reasoning. Deductive reasoning means moving from a general idea to a specific one.

metaphysics—The branch of philosophy dealing with the nature of being and existence. Also, the underlying principles that form the basis of a field of knowledge.

Peripatetics—Philosophers at Aristotle's Lyceum. Possibly so called from their habit of walking as they taught. *Peripateo* was Greek for "to walk."

philosophy—From the ancient Greek *philos* meaning love and s*ophia* meaning wisdom. The branch of knowledge dealing with the systematic examination of basic ideas such as truth, existence, and reality.

polis—An ancient Greek city-state.

physiology—The branch of biology that deals with the internal workings of living things.

sophist—Greek "teachers of wisdom." Their subjects included mathematics, antiquities, and linguistics.

syllogism—Deductive argument. Reasoning moving from a general idea to a specific one.

FURTHER READING

Books

Cooper, Sharon Katz. *Aristotle: Philosopher, Teacher, and Scientist*. Minneapolis, Minn.: Compass Point Books, 2007.

Isle, Mick. *Aristotle: Pioneering Philosopher and Founder of the Lyceum*. New York: Rosen Publishing Group, 2006.

Nardo, Don. *Ancient Greece*. Detroit, Mich.: Lucent Books, 2006.

Peppas, Lynn. *Life in Ancient Greece*. New York: Crabtree Publishing, 2005.

Williams, Jean. *Empire of Ancient Greece*. New York: Facts On File, 2005.

Internet Addresses

Works by Aristotle, *The Internet Classics Archive*
http://classics.mit.edu/Browse/browse-Aristotle.html

Aristotle Biography, *University of California Museum of Paleontology*
http://www.ucmp.berkeley.edu/history/aristotle.html

Aristotle Biography, *The Internet Encyclopedia of Philosophy*
http://www.iep.utm.edu/a/aristotl.htm

INDEX